How to Publish and Sell Your Article on the Kindle

12 Beginner Tips for Short Documents

By Kate Harper

~

For Writers & Poets

CONTENTS

⟨?⟩

f ⟨?⟩

INTRODUCTION

I believe an exciting opportunity for writers today is "Kindle Articles": Short documents, similar to printed magazine articles, published on the Amazon Store for the Kindle.

Until I started selling hundreds of articles a month, I didn't realize there was a ready, accessible market for short documents, or how many people were interested in buying them. I learned that a writer doesn't have to publish an entire book in order to receive royalties for their work. I think articles are the new secret "sweet spot" of the e-Reader publishing market.

There is a large amount of information available on how to publish e-Books, but little attention is given to selling articles. A writer should have specific knowledge about how to create effective article-length documents such as: how to price them, how long they should be, the best way to describe them on the Amazon Store, and how to give the customer a good value.

The advantages of publishing articles are:

1) They allow writers to receive monthly royalties instead of flat fees.

2) They are displayed next to books on the Amazon and Nook Store websites.

3) And, because their price is typically much lower than books, they are a comparable bargain when sitting next to a book.

You don't need to know HTML, use special software, or pay fees in order to publish an article. You can easily write, convert, upload and publish your article by simply using a word processor.

Most of the information in this book comes from my own experience of buying and selling Kindle Articles. I am also active in the Kindle publishing support communities, forums and newsgroups, and I have seen many of the problems writers face when trying to sell short documents.

This book contains many recommendations that distinguish the differences between publishing articles and books, along with how to increase sales, prepare documents in the simplest way, and format them simultaneously for multiple devices, such as the Barnes and Noble Nook. The recommendations are also applicable to Amazon "Singles" which are short stories, memoirs, essays and articles ranging from 5,000-30,000 words.

I hope you find these tips helpful, and I would enjoy hearing about your own experience publishing articles for e-Readers.

TIP 1: THE FIRST PAGE

Only Put 4 Things on Your First Page.

Publishing guidelines for most e-Readers instruct you to put your front matter on separate pages (i.e. a table of contents, title, copyright, acknowledgements, dedication, preface, prologue, and publisher contact information). By doing this, you can easily add many pages to the beginning of your document before the reader arrives at your main content.

This practice is actually a *disadvantage* when publishing e-Reader Articles. Because the Amazon Bookstore offers free samples of books and articles that are auto-generated from about the first 10% of the beginning of your document, this uses up precious sample space. For a book-length document, this might include the front matter plus one chapter, which is fine as a sample. However, for a Kindle article 10% may not even allow your reader to reach the first paragraph of your content.

If your article sample ends up consisting of only your front matter, a potential buyer can't read the beginning of the content, reducing the odds they will buy it. Therefore, put most of the front matter at the end of your article instead of the beginning.

Consider limiting your front matter to four basic items, and put them all on one page.

• Title of Article

• Author Name

• Topic List or "Table of Contents" (TOC)

• Copyright

Here's an example from one of my current Kindle articles. It saves document space and allows the reader of the sample text to receive more of the actual content:

~ SAMPLE ~

Seven Mistakes Greeting Card Writers Make

By Kate Harper, Product Designer

Cards as Relationships • Creating Cards for Enemies • Limiting the Market • Using Adjectives • Putting Syrup on • Being Too Literary • Articles • Interviews

It doesn't take fancy fonts or special design skills to make a page like this. You can simply use the following format and it will look good on a Kindle screen:

• Insert a carriage return before the title.

• Use 12-point bold type for the title.

• Use 10-point italic type for the author name.

• Use 12-point regular type for the TOC topics.

• Use one font: Times New Roman.

• Insert bullets between topics with a space on each side of the bullet. Type in bullets from the keyboard by hand with a space on each side (option+8 on the Mac). Don't use the auto-generated bullets from pull down menus.

• Use 10-point type for the copyright.

You can link your TOC topic list to the associated locations in your article, similar to how book chapters are linked to TOC entries in Kindle books. (See Appendix A)

I believe the amount of actual article text in the

free sample is ultimately very important to the reader's purchasing decision. If you have a very long article or one with several sections, it's probably Ok to use a separate page for a TOC. But if you aren't sure, err on the side of giving your reader more free content. Ideally you want 500 words or more in the free sample.

Moving front matter to the end of the article is also helpful for readers who find it tiresome to page through 15-20 screens just to reach the main content.

TIP 2: IMAGES IN FRONT

Avoid Inserting Images at the Beginning.

Unless you have a long article (20-30 pages) or the subject of your article relies heavily on images, it's probably best to avoid inserting images at the beginning of your document since they use up too much of the initial 10% of the space that Amazon will use to generate the content for your free sample. This doesn't mean you can't have images in your article; just add them after the sample pages, further along in the document.

One exception to this rule might be if your subject is visual, such as an article about digital photography. In this case, it might be nice to have a picture in the introduction to set a tone for your subject matter.

TIP 3: WORD PROCESSOR

Keep it Simple: Put Your Text in A Word Processor.

In order to publish your article on a Kindle, you first need to prepare the document in a form the Kindle can read, which the Amazon website lists as the following file types:

Zipped HTML (.zip)

Word (.doc)

Adobe PDF (.pdf)

ePub (.epub)

Plain Text (.txt)

MobiPocket (.mobi and .prc)

When I started publishing Kindle and Nook articles, I experimented with these choices, read books on Kindle formatting, participated in newsgroups and community help forums, used conversion software and coding by hand in HTML. While there are pros and cons of each, I believe the easiest way to prepare your article, especially for a beginner, is to use a word processor such as MS Word or free software such as OpenOffice http://www.openoffice.org/ and save it in the .doc file type.

The advantages are:

1) Formatting is easy since most people are familiar with word processors.

2) There are fewer problems when uploading the same document to multiple e-Readers.

3) You can insert images without attaching separate image files.

4) There isn't a technical barrier of having to learn a markup language, like HTML.

5) The results are more consistent (if you stay with basic formatting) on multiple devices.

6) You don't have to use conversion software.

The downside of word processors is they generally add more unnecessary HTML code behind the scenes, but since articles are much shorter and less complex than books, there is little downside to using them.

Note: When using MS Word or OpenOffice, make sure to save your document in a .doc format. Avoid saving it as a .docx or .odt file types, since some e-Readers don't accept those formats.

TIP 4: FORMATTING TEXT

Use Kindle-Friendly Formatting.

Book layouts, especially those layouts inherited from a traditional, printed book can be complex, and converting an existing book for the Kindle can be quite involved. The book's layout can specify chapter breaks, partially blank pages, multiple sized images, page numbers, drop caps, line breaks, special word layout for poetry, tab indents, etc.

I recommend, at least initially, keeping your article formatting simple.

Here are some "rules of thumb" for doing that when using a word processor. Adhering to these practices will decrease the chances of problems, and increase consistency across multiple e-Readers.

Formatting Rules of Thumb:

• Start with an unformatted document, i.e. in "plain text." You can do this by making a copy of your original article and pasting it into a text editor in plain text mode. You can also use the "clear formatting," function often under the "edit" menus in most word processors.

• Remove page numbers, special margins, headers, footers, tabs or anything else beyond default formatting.

• Prepare the document single-spaced.

• Try to do most of your text editing, spell checking and other content changes before you do any formatting. Avoid formatting your document while writing it.

• Try to stick with the basics: Bold, underline, italic and left, center and right alignment.

• Avoid changing the format multiple times on the same text. For example, going back and forth from bold to italic ten different times.

• Opt for the font "Times New Roman" and use it for the entire document.

• Use even numbered font sizes, and try to stick with only 10, 12 and 14-point type.

• Avoid using pull-down menus to insert type. Instead, enter text from the keyboard. For example, if you want to change a sentence from lower to upper case, don't use text transformation functions on your toolbar. Rather, erase and retype the text in upper case. If you want a numbered list, use your keyboard to enter the number, and avoid auto-generated list functions offered in your word processor.

• Don't use the Table of Contents functions in your word processor to create and format title lists.

Instead refer to Appendix A on simple ways to insert TOC topic lists, internal links, anchor tags and bookmarks.

• Don't use hard or soft carriage returns two times in a row unless you want a larger than expected gap of empty space on the Kindle screen. (To learn how to deal with unexpected or unattractive gaps of white space between sections of your article, see Appendix C for different formatting options.)

Later, if you decide you want to explore more sophisticated formatting options, I recommend reading the Building Your Book for Kindle (free) or purchase *Kindle Formatting* by Joshua Tallent. You can also read the *Amazon Knowledge Base* and Community Forums, Barnes and Noble Nook *Pubit Help Board*, and *Pubit Support page* (Also see Resource List).

TIP 5: ADDING LINKS

Take Advantage of Links.

My experience in buying and reading Kindle articles is they tend to have many more hyperlinks than books. One reason for this might be that eBooks tend to be reformatted from a printed document, and they weren't written with hyperlinks in mind, nor did the publisher plan on the reader "clicking through" to a website.

Kindle articles, on the other hand, usually have

not appeared in print, and the authors tend to include hyperlinks as a feature of the document. The result is the article is more interactive than the average book.

Links are a great feature to add to your article because they help you offer timely edits and updates. Even though some e-Readers have slow or limited web surfing abilities, it's only a matter of time before they all allow us to click on links and easily take us to web pages.

With links also comes an extra responsibility for the writer to test and update links periodically. I have found that businesses and blogs will sometimes remove links or change them and it can be a challenge to keep up with edits. Luckily, most readers are forgiving, and I am always grateful when they write to me and alert me to a dead link. Since continual updating of certain types of information might be important in your article, you might consider creating links that point directly to a webpage or blog that is updated, rather than re-editing your article and uploading it frequently.

For example, if you have a section in your article that lists free online classes, you could add additional classes as you become aware of them, on an external webpage or blog page. This way, you can update the information in a few minutes on the blog, rather than republish your article frequently. (If you don't want to pay a monthly fee to host a blog or website, here are several places you can do this for free: *Top 10 Free Online Blogging Platforms* http://sixrevisions.com/tools/top-free-online-blogging/)

If you do edit and upload your article often, please note that *Amazon overwrites the article and does not remove it from the store.* Therefore, you do not have to worry about your article disappearing from the store at any time. Because Amazon takes 1-2 days to evaluate and upload the new version, you will have to wait before you upload additional versions.

If you make major changes to your document and want to give updated copies to all your prior customers, you can submit this request to Amazon (see: *Notifying Customers of Book Updates* https://kdp.amazon.com/self-publishing/help?topicId=A1RGGPBKDR1BPZ)

Search Engine Optimization in web design usually discourages adding links that lead visitors off a site, but unlike websites, links in Kindle articles have no real downside. If your reader abandons your article for a website, they will eventually return, because they've made a financial investment in it, and it will still be sitting on their Kindle when they return.

TIP 6: ADDING IMAGES

Use Images After the Sample Section.

Printed articles often have images and readers usually expect them. The main thing to remember, especially for short articles, is to try and put your images after the free sample section unless the subject of your article is visual, such as photography, design, or instructional diagrams.

Since articles tend to be non-fiction and can be

technical, I think it helps to add more images when explaining complicated topics. The challenge with the Kindle screen is anything with small text, like a street map, might not be very readable. In a case like this, blow up the image by scanning it at a higher resolution and possibly limit how much of the map the reader will see at any one time.

My experience is that graphics with high contrast and photographs of people tend to display OK, but the best approach is to experiment by creating a separate document with various images, upload them onto your Kindle to preview them, and see what they look like. Then you can choose the best ones.

There is much detailed information on image optimization for e-Readers. The following recommendations are my "rules of thumb" for simplicity sake, and for ease of remembering. Detailed Kindle recommendations, which have minimum sizes, maximum sizes, image format options and other recommendations, can be viewed on the Amazon Web page and on the resource list.

Image Tips:

• Try to keep each image size around 100 K.

• Use jpg or gif's.

• Use color or black and white. If you have a color image, don't change it to black and white or a grey scale because some e-Readers have color screens.

• When inserting images, don't cut and paste them into your article. Instead insert images by using the INSERT menu on your toolbar. (See Appendix B)

• Center-align all images. Don't use any special alignment like having text flow around the image.

• It's attractive to insert a page break before and after images, especially if there is a caption you want to be snug next to your photo. Just be aware that not all e-Readers recognize page breaks in word processors, such as the Nook. Instead, use "section breaks" that break to the next page, (in place of page breaks). They work on both the Kindle and the Nook.

• Aim for images sizes approximately 600x800

pixels. Amazon will automatically reduce larger sizes.

TIP 7: BEGINNING AND END

Take a Second Look at the Beginning and End

The beginning and end of e-Reader articles are unique, compared to a print article. Since the beginning of your article is where Amazon offers about 10% of text for the free sample, think carefully about what you put there. A good beginning offers an overview of the topics that will be covered, why they matter, and entices the reader to want to read the rest of the article.

The ending is also important to review because with short Kindle articles, the end can arrive abruptly and the reader may not be prepared for it. This is an electronic document issue: since you can't see or feel pages in your hand, and the amount of text displayed at any one time is limited, you can lose the sense of how far along you are in the article.

Even though the Kindle has location numbers at the bottom of the page, some people do not check them often. They can also be displayed as number "ranges" (i.e. 105-120) or a percentage instead of a page number. Unless you are watching these numbers carefully, you may not realize how fast you are moving through a document, and if an article has several pages of footnotes at the end, you may think the article has fifteen more Kindle pages, and you may be surprised to find it only has one.

One way to alert the reader the end is coming is notify them with "Conclusion" or "Final Tips" or some other text preparations so they know "the end is near!"

TIP 8: ADD A RESOURCE LIST

Add a Resource List & Author Section.

I've found one of the most important sections of Kindle articles is a resource list. I've received positive feedback from my readers that my resource lists are a great value to them, and they alone, were worth the price of the article. This is a great place to add links and your personal recommendations.

Here is a list of resources you might offer. Try to

recommend things you have actually used, purchased and that are specifically related to the subject matter of your article. Avoid inserting laundry lists of extraneous information.

Resources Lists

- Links to Books.

- Relevant Online Classes and Tutorials on Your Topic.

- Video, Audio Podcasts or Interviews You've Heard.

- Organizations, User Groups, Facebook Groups, Linkedin Groups, Yahoo Groups, and Forums you've Participated in.

- Free apps, or Software Downloads You've Used.

- Checklists, Shopping Lists, Packing Lists, Material Lists or To Do Lists.

- Graphics, Tables or Questionnaires.

• Online Stores for Specialty Items Discussed in Your Article.

• How-To Instructions.

• Freebies

Author Info

It's helpful to put an Author Information page at the end of your article so people can contact you, your website, or know more about you.

• Education, Experience or Qualifications.

• Photo

• Contact Information: Phone, Mailing Address, Email Address, Website, Twitter Address.

• Your Social Networks such as a Blog RSS Feed, Podcasts you broadcast, LinkedIn Groups, or Facebook Pages.

• Freebies you are offering to Your Readers.

• Testimonials

• A List of Other Items You've Published.

• Invitation For Feedback.

• Private Link to a Webpage Just For Your Readers.

Since this information is at the end of the article, you can also add the front matter you did not include on your first page, such as acknowledgements, credits, etc.

TIP 9: UPLOADING YOUR ARTICLE

Special Tips for Uploading Articles.

Besides preparing your document file, you will also need additional items in order to upload your article and publish it in the Amazon and Nook Stores. While many of these items are the same things you'll need to upload a book, and information on filling out the form is explained in detail in other publications and online, I want to point out three specific things on the form you might want to make a note of during this process.

1. The Book Cover

Besides preparing your document file, you will also need additional items in order to upload your article and publish it in the Amazon and Nook Stores. Many of these items are the same things you'll need to upload a book, and information on filling out the form is explained in detail in other publications and online. I want to point out three things you might want to make a note of during the upload process, that is specific to articles.

1. Book Cover: Try to avoid creating book covers from 3-D e-Book templates you often find free on different websites (sample below). They don't match the 2-D covers in the Amazon store, and 3-D covers tend to look like thick books, which might confuse the buyer into thinking they are buying a book and not an article. This is an example of a 3-D book template:

Note: Your book cover will be displayed in the Amazon store. When uploading a cover, use a .tiff or .jpg image around 900 x 1200 pixels at 72 dpi, ideally in color. Specifications change periodically. Check the help page at Amazon KDP.

If you don't know how to make a book cover or can't afford to pay a professional book designer, you can search the Kindle Community Forums for low cost covers by independent artists. You can also make your own by using my free 'book cover tutorial for non-designers' I created for my readers (info at the end of this book).

2. Article Description: For the article description that will appear on the Amazon Store, you want to make it clear your document is an article and not a book, by listing the number of pages and word count.

Note: The article description may take 3 days to appear after you publish the book, and the book might take 2 days to appear on the Amazon website, so you might wait 5 days before all your information is updated on the Amazon Store.

3. Tags: You have the option of adding search tags for your article. The search tags are a good place to highlight that your document is an article and not a book. So you could add the word "article" in the tag list.   Here is a good article on how to pick ebook tags: http://mlouisalocke.com/2011/10/24/categories-key-words-and-tags-oh-my-why-should-an-author-care/

If you want a detailed overview of step-by-step instructions on how to go through the Amazon submission process, watch this free Amazon video: https://kdp.amazon.com/self-publishing/help?topicId=A2M7MM0UP7PHK0

TIP 10: ARTICLE PRICING

Make Your Price Attractive.

I believe that determining a price for your Kindle article depends on three things: the length of the article, the value of the content, and if the article is newly published.

As someone who has purchased many articles, I believe they should be at least ten pages in length for me to feel it is a good value (a page being defined as single spaced page in a typical word processor), and depending on whether it has images, the word count might range from 3,000-6,000 words. A document this size would probably sell for 99-cents, the minimum price you can charge for any type of Kindle document (exclusions are public domain and publisher promos).

A good formula for pricing an article is:

• 10 pages (3,000-5,000 words) or more = 99 cents

• 20 pages (5,000-10,000 words) or more = $1.99

• 30 pages or (10,000-30,000 words) or more = $2.99

This calculates to about ten cents per page. Beyond 30 pages, this formula starts to break down, since you are then entering into the territory of books. It is not reasonable to attempt to sell a 300-page book for 10-cents a page since a $30 book is way beyond the typical price of $9.99 for a Kindle book.

I believe the biggest opportunity in publishing articles is the price point of $2.99 because your royalties more than double once you reach that price threshold. Anything priced under $2.99 only offers a 35% royalty.

Therefore, writing and selling a high quality article at least 30 pages in length is an ideal goal to aim for. Receiving a 70% royalty for each $2.99 article will bring in more than $2 each. If you only sold one article a day for a month, this revenue can add up quickly, and 10 articles a day would bring in over $600. You can see why selling articles for the Kindle provides an income way beyond what a magazine might offer.

I also think it's important to keep an article under $3 because there is a psychological barrier customers reach when it comes to buying short documents over the price of $2.99, especially when they can find a good selection of books that start around $4.00 and $5.00. It's better to err on the side of a satisfied customer, than overcharging them for mediocre content or shorter articles than they expected.

When starting out, you might consider publishing a new article for 99-cents just to become familiar with the process, and then see what kind of response you receive. If you find you are selling ten articles a day at 99-cents, perhaps you underestimated the value of your article. You might experiment with inching up the price to $1.29 and see if you still get the same response. If you do increase the price, I think it's always a good practice to add something to the article to give it more value. It's good to start with a low price, and then let your document gain momentum. For the same royalty profit, it's better to get six buyers at 99-cents than one buyer at $2.99 because your article will move higher up the sales ranks, get more exposure in the store, and the opportunity for getting reviews increase.

Regarding valuable content, unless you are a famous author, a short piece of fiction may have a less perceived value to a customer than an article on marketing cell phone apps. You need to plan accordingly and experiment with different types of article content in regard to pricing. Also, it can take several months before your article catches on or people can find it.

In one of my articles, I found that my readers really valued a list of contacts I included. Even though this was not a long article, I was able to sell it at a higher price point.

TIP 11: STORE DESCRIPTION

Include Four Items in Your Store Description.

When I've purchased publications from the Amazon Bookstore, I've found it very disappointing to think I am buying a book, and it turns out to only be an article, and this points to a problem I continue to see on e-book Stores: *Article writers often do not include the length of their document in the store description.*

If someone buys your article and thinks they are getting a book, it can lead to dissatisfied customers leaving negative reviews. That can harm sales. But there's also another uncertainty: if a customer sees a 99-cent item in the Amazon store, they might guess it is not a book, and wonder why it is so inexpensive. But if the description doesn't specifically state length, a sale can easily be lost because the customer is uncertain about what he is getting.

(Ebook stores often provide the KB's size of article in the description, but knowing a document is 60KB doesn't help the average reader, because they can't calculate how many pages of text or images that is.)

I recommend including the following items in your Amazon Store product descriptions:

1. The first sentence should identify the product up front as an "article."

2. If your article is short (10-15 pages), include the word [article] in brackets after the title.

3. Include the page length of the article (for a

single spaced, 8 ½ x11 sized standard page in a word processor).

4. At the end of the description, include a word count in parenthesis.

Adding the word count is helpful for people who'd rather determine document sizes by the number of words, especially if the article states it has several images. I also think it's better to add a word count at the end of the description instead of the beginning, since putting both numbers together in the first sentence makes the customer stumble through too many numbers to get to the description.

Here is an example of how you might write a product description for e-Reader stores:

Cruise Ship Tricks [Article]

In this 14-page article you will learn tips on how to break rules on a cruise ship and save money, avoid bad entertainment, pack one bag, not dress up, and what to bring that isn't in the brochure, and best of all, how to take advantage of what's available.

Also included are personal recommendations for budget booking, specialty cruises, solo cruising, best kept secrets, and where to find good cruise reviews. Written by a frugal traveler who has been on dozens of cruises around the world, and has booked trips with several different cruise lines (Article: 3,500 Words).

~

You might consider describing your article as a "booklet" instead of an article, especially if your document is over 20 pages and is instructional in nature, such as a How-To topic.

While this above example is short, your description can be much longer. Consider including information about you (the author) and your qualifications or experience.

TIP 12: SELLING YOUR ARTICLE

Use the Best Practices to Sell Articles.

I find the best ways to sell a Kindle article are to:

1) Select good tags.

2) Choose appropriate categories in the "category section" when filling out the form.

3) Offer a lot of content in the sample pages.

4) Write a clear description of your article on the Amazon Store listing.

5) Start out by offering it at a very low price, ideally 99 cents. You can always change it later.

6) Create an attractive book cover to post on the Amazon Store. Very Important: *Make sure the title stands out when it is reduced to the size of an inch wide.* You can do this by making large dark words on a light background, and incorporate a colorful photo. (For a free pdf on how to make your own book cover, see "freebie for my readers" at the end of this book).

7) Consider enrolling in Amazon's KDP select http://kdp.amazon.com/self-publishing/KDPSelect This option allows you to offer promos to readers and give your article away. Giving an article away has a lot of advantages since you can increase your ranking and also expose your readers to other articles you've written. I did this with my first short story and it reached #23 in science fiction top sellers in one day! Not bad for someone who has never published a science fiction short story before. Just make sure you read the restrictions. If you use KDP, you are not allowed to sell your book on other sites during that

time.

8) Submit your article to Amazon's "Kindle Singles" program. The advantage of being accepted is that your article will be additionally marketed in the exclusive "Singles" category. This section highlights short documents that Amazon recommends to readers. Here are guidelines on how to apply to be a "Kindle Singles" author:

- Your document must be 5,000 to 30,000 words

- The price must be: $0.99 to $4.99

- Your work must be original work, and not previously published in other formats or publications.

- It must be a self-contained work, and not chapters excerpted from a longer work.

- It cannot be published on any public website in its entirety

- You can send reports, essays, memoirs, narratives, and short stories. Avoid sending how-to manuals, public domain works, reference books, travel guides, or children's books.

•Send submissions to mailto:kindle-singles@amazon.com and include the title, ASIN, and a brief summary.

For more information on submitting manuscripts for a Kindle Single, see: http://www.amazon.com/gp/feature.html?ie=UTF8&docId=1000700491

Also listen to this interview with Amazon editor David Blum. He discusses how documents and articles are selected for this exclusive section of the Amazon store. See the Kindle Chronicles Podcast #169, http://www.thekindlechronicles.com/2011/10/29/tkc-169-david-blum/

9) Publish your article directly with Barnes and Noble for the Nook. Just like on Amazon you can publish your article in the Barnes and Noble Bookstore at http://pubit.barnesandnoble.com/pubit_app/bn?t=pi_reg_home

10) Publish your article with *Smashwords* (http://www.smashwords.com/). The thing I like about Smashwords is they distribute your article to multiple publishing markets including: the Apple ibookstore, Barnes and Noble Bookstore, Kobo, Diesel ebookstore, and the Sony Reader Store. Some stores and publishers will not accept independent articles directly from an author, but Smashwords has a special relationship with each of one of them and can do it for you. This is a good way to get your article in the popular Apple Computer ibookstore.

Smashwords will give you a free ISBN number and distribute your article for free. They take a small royalty for their services, but it is well worth it. Otherwise, you might not even get access to publishing your article to some of these outlets.

They also offer two excellent free ebooks: 1) The *Smashwords Style Guide* and 2) *Smashwords Book Marketing Guide*. The Smashwords Style Guide (http://www.smashwords.com/books/view/52) will help you through their publishing process and teach you how to format documents for their distribution and the Smashwords Book Marketing Guide (http://www.smashwords.com/books/view/305) is the best book I've ever seen on creative ways to market your ebook.

Smashwords will give you a free ISBN number and distribute your article for free. They take a small royalty for their services, but it is well worth it. Otherwise, you might not even get access to publishing your article to some of these outlets.

They also offer two excellent free ebooks: 1) The "Style Guide" (http://www.smashwords.com/books/view/52) will help you through their publishing process and teach you how to format documents for their distribution and 2) the "Smashwords Book Marketing Guide" (http://www.smashwords.com/books/view/305) is the best book I've ever seen on creative ways to market your ebook.

11. Consider taking a step up and consider publishing your article as a printed book through Createspace (https://www.createspace.com/). If your article is lengthy, or you want to publish poetry or a cookbook, you can have it published in print, and sold in the Amazon Bookstore. I was surprised to find that

one of my articles was long enough to printed in book form. It made me realize that a lot of printed books are really the size of long articles.

Createspace will print, publish and distribute your book for free. All you need to do is purchase a proof copy for about $10 so you can see your book in print before you release it to the public.

Createspace has free templates and you can do it all yourself, but they also provide editing, designing and marketing for a reasonable price.

12. Offer copies to libraries. Here is a great article that discusses the benefits of giving away your ebook (or article) to libraries: *Ebooks for Libraries* http://jakonrath.blogspot.com/2012/08/ebooks-for-libraries.html

~

I did not do any marketing on my first 99-cent article, yet I watched it promote itself. I believe this is because I experimented with tweaking the description and changing tags and categories so they better represented what I was selling. I also included my email address in the article so that readers could easily give me feedback for improvements.

Another important thing to do is let people know your article exists through social media. I've had the best response by displaying my article book cover image (from the Amazon store), on the sidebar of my blog, with a direct link to Amazon site for purchasing.

My experience is, it takes an article a few months to catch on, and then it seems to start selling itself because your rankings go up and the article gets a more prominent placement in the Amazon Store. Being on Amazon is comparable to having a free advertising department, since they do such a massive business and have a lot of customers who browse for new publications.

Another good way to sell articles is to let your readers know you have other articles. List them with your author information. If they enjoyed your first article, chances are they will purchase more.

CONCLUSION

I'd like to end this book with my story of how I began publishing articles on the Kindle. Since I have some technical skills, I volunteered to help a friend publish her poetry book for the Kindle, but before I posted it, I wanted to practice with a test document first so I didn't make any mistakes with her book. I published a travel article I had on my computer; with no expectations that anyone would even notice it was available. I was surprised to discover I received a few sales the first month, but then was amazed when sales kept increasing each month to the point where I was selling the article about ten times a day.

After that, I started to publish articles on my area of expertise, gift and product design. I published parts of a manual I'd written on the greeting card business and pulled content from my design blog. Sales were strong because information on the gift design wholesale business is hard to find. Very few books have been written on this subject.

Publishing articles on the Kindle has been an enjoyable experience and I believe there are many untapped possibilities for writers who have enthusiasm for all kinds of topics.

With Kindle articles and Kindle "Singles," the future of print magazine publishing could change dramatically. For an author to receive recurring royalties for articles is unusual, and it's another demonstration of how the digital age offers new opportunities for people from all walks of life.

I believe the future looks bright, especially for people who want to live and work in the creative sphere. Now writers have control over when, where, and how their work is published. After all, *you* are the best agent, when it comes to representing your own work.

APPENDIX

Appendix A:

How to Create TOC Links in a Word Processor

(aka: Internal Links, Bookmark, Anchor Tags)

Using MS Word

1. Don't use any automatic features that generate a Table of Contents. Ignore them, since you are going to insert your links differently.

2. Select the location in your document where you want the reader to go "to" when they click the link.

In the example below I want to link to the packing list at the end of my cruise article. I have put my blinking curser next to the "Packing Checklist" title. Do not highlight anything; just make sure you have a blinking insertion bar.

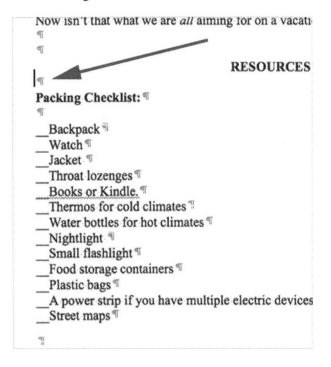

Now isn't that what we are *all* aiming for on a vacati

RESOURCES

Packing Checklist:

__Backpack
__Watch
__Jacket
__Throat lozenges
__Books or Kindle.
__Thermos for cold climates
__Water bottles for hot climates
__Nightlight
__Small flashlight
__Food storage containers
__Plastic bags
__A power strip if you have multiple electric devices
__Street maps

3. Pull down the INSERT menu and select BOOKMARK

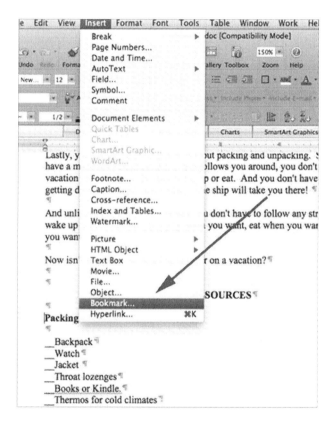

4. A bookmark dialogue box will open and then you will need to give your bookmark a name. In my example, I named the bookmark "packing_list". After you name the bookmark, click ADD.

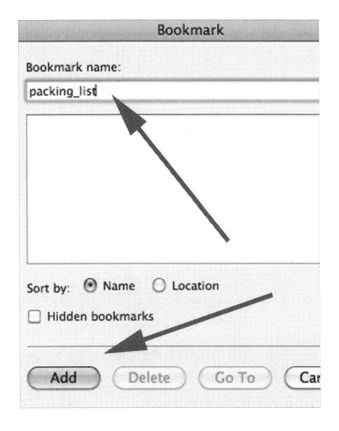

5. You should notice an "I" bar symbol appear in the location of the bookmark.

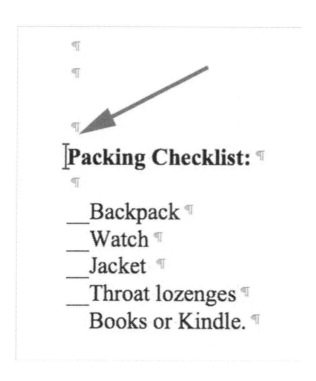

6. Now, go to your TOC or to the location where you want the hyperlink to be (it will direct the reader to your "packing_list" bookmark). I went to the beginning of my TOC topic list and chose the "Packing Checklist" topic at the beginning of my Document.

Now highlight the text where you want a highlighted link, and pull down the INSERT menu and select HYPERLINK (command+K on Mac).

This will open an INSERT HYPERLINK titled dialogue box.

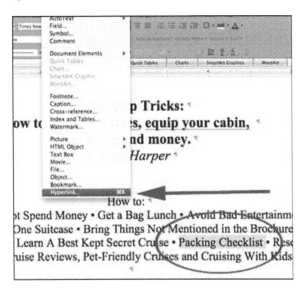

7. There are four things to do in this next section.

a) First, select the DOCUMENT tab in between the WEBPAGE and EMAIL ADDRESS tab.

b) Second, on the ANCHOR label, click LOCATE. This will open a second, overlapping dialogue box.

c) Select the triangle on the left side of BOOKMARKS and it will open up a list of bookmarks you have made. In this sample document, we only have one bookmark, "packing-list", on the list.

d) Select it and then click OK to close the dialogue box.

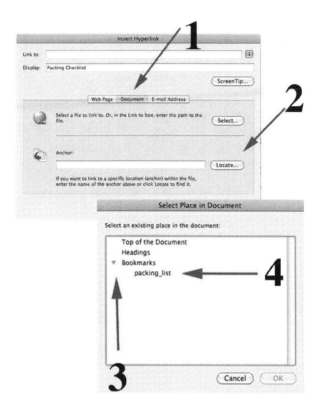

8. Notice the text in the TOC topic list is highlighted, and it is now an internal link. Clicking on

this link, will take you to the place bookmarked. In this case, it is the packing list at the end of the article.

You don't have to limit yourself to TOC links, you can link to other places in your document, such as appendixes, or other references later in your article.

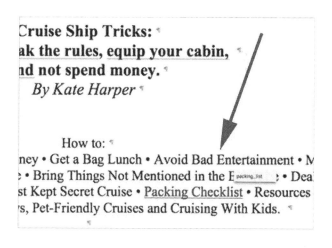

9. Repeat this process for any internal links you want in your article.

10. The Kindle also has special bookmark names that do not have "highlighted" links you can see, rather they are markers for the Kindle device, and so

reader can find your TOC and the beginning of your document when they are reading your article. They have special names: "TOC" and "start." Repeat only steps 1 through 5 and these two bookmarks to the beginning of your document (without the quotations).

You might want to put the TOC bookmark at the beginning of your TOC topic list and add the word "start" as a bookmark at the very beginning of your article. If you do not have a book cover, it is possible these two bookmarks will end up on the same page. That's OK. You mainly want the reader to be able to go to these locations easily while they are reading your article.

Appendix B:

How to Insert Images in a Kindle Document

Do not cut and paste images into your MS Word Document. Instead, insert them through the pull down menus.

1. Put your cursor where you want the image to appear. I have chosen to insert a travel photo in between the following two paragraphs.

To do that, I have inserted three carriage returns (recommended) and intend to insert the photo on the middle carriage return.

owns the jewelry store they are driving you to.

If you are truly set on an excursion tour, only pick one or two that y
go on, or choose one you could never do in the United States. For
engineering tour of the Panama Canal is logistically difficult to arra
cruise.

I strongly believe that by interfacing with communities and foreign
without being separated by the window of a tour bus, is going to gi
satisfying travel experience at significantly reduced cost; additional
stories to share with your tablemates.

2. Don't Spend Money On The Ship

While almost everything is free on board, you might end up spendi
unnecessarily. If you like alcoholic drinks, sodas, gambling, gift sh
salons or bingo, you will probably rack up charges on your credit ca
things don't interest you that much, you can get away with having a
the end of the trip.

2. Now pull down the INSERT menu and select PICTURE, which will open a submenu. Select FROM FILE. You will now need to find the location of your image on your computer.

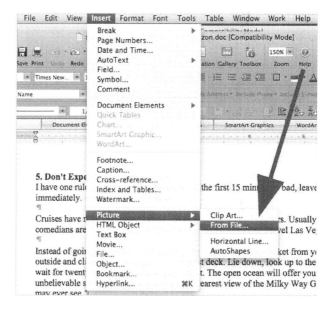

3. Locate your image and press the INSERT button in the lower right.

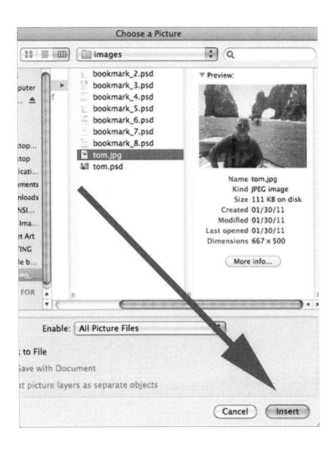

4. My image appeared between the paragraphs. Your image should also appear in your document.

Now center the image. You should always center images in Kindle article documents since they look more attractive. You can also add a 10-point size font and put a caption under the photo.

Appendix C

Blank Space Between Paragraphs

One of the biggest problems you will probably encounter when uploading a document to the Kindle that was created on a word processor, are large space gaps that can appear between paragraphs. This gap is created during the conversion process where HTML paragraph < p > tags are replacing carriage returns, and it causes the gap.

This can be a very frustrating experience if you have formatted your document perfectly, but when you upload it, it looks quite different.

If you are having this experience, one rule of thumb is to never use two carriage returns in a row.

One would think soft carriage returns would solve the problem, but my experience has been that the gap still remains.

The simplest way to resolve this problem (other than editing your document in html) is to use line space formatting. It is normally found in the paragraph formatting section of your word processor, and the Barnes and Noble Nook formatting guidelines recommend this.

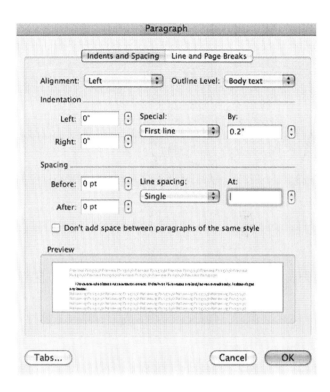

You don't have to try to eliminate the blank space, but if you want to, aim for one of the following, which increase in complexity by number.

...end of former paragraph.

A. 1 CARRIGE RETURN

This is what the default MS Word document looks like with one carriage return between former paragraph, title and the following text.

B. 2 HARD RETURNS

This is what the default MS Word document looks like with two carriage returns between former paragraph, title and the following text. (soft returns have same result)

C. 1 RETURN PLUS 12 PT LINE

This is what a title looks like if you format the entire document with 12-point line spacing after paragraphs.

D. SAMPLE C PLUS 0 PT TITLE

This is what a title looks like if you format the entire document with a 12-point line after the paragraph ends, and format 0 point line on the titles only.

E. SAMPLE D CENTERED

This is what a title looks like if you format the entire document with a 12-point line after the paragraph, format 0 point line on the titles, then center it.

F. SAMPLE D PLUS 2 PT INDENT

This is what a title looks like if you format the entire document with a 2 point first line indent, a 12-point line after the paragraph, and 0 point line on the titles.

The next line looks like this.

G. SAMPLE F CENTERED

This is what a title looks like if you format the entire document with a 2 point first line indent, and 0 point line after paragraphs.

Then you go back to the titles, and add a 12-point line after the last sentence of the previous section.

C. Format the entire document with 12-point line spacing after paragraphs.

D. Format the entire document with a 12-point line after the paragraph ends, and format 0 point line on the titles only.

E. Format the entire document with a 12-point line after the paragraph, format 0 point line on the titles, then center it.

F. Format the entire document with a 2 point first line indent, a 12-point line after the paragraph, and 0 point line on the titles.

G Format the entire document with a 2 point first line indent, and 0 point line after paragraphs. Then you go back to the titles, and add a 12-point line after the last sentence of the previous section.

Depending on how many title sections you have, and how long your document is, will determine which style you prefer to undertake.

Normally, bold font weight and capital letters tend to look like they are screaming on a printed document in a word processor, but when you upload them onto a Kindle, the bold is not as strong as one might expect, and the capital letters aren't as jarring.

You might want to experiment with title case and bold font weight to see which one looks best with your content.

Appendix D

Publishing on the Nook

If you are going to publish your article on the Kindle, you should consider also publishing it on the Nook and possibly other e-Readers.

One advantage of the Nook is that it has a color screen and provides opportunities for people who are publishing articles that have a lot of colored imagery. For example, Will Terry's blog article reported how the Nook was a great opportunity to publish his own children's books and believes this could be a tremendous opportunity for children's book authors and artists.

Having worked as a designer in the art licensing profession myself, I know the children's book industry is extremely competitive and it is very difficult to get your book published through traditional print publishers. He seems to have found his niche among Nook readers. I believe the same opportunities exist for articles that require a lot of colored imagery such as gardening, cooking or photography. The potential topics are endless.

For more information on how to publish on the Nook, see the Resource List at the end of this book.

Here is what the previewer looks like for the Nook when you upload your article. (More on previewing in Appendix E).

< Previous | Next >

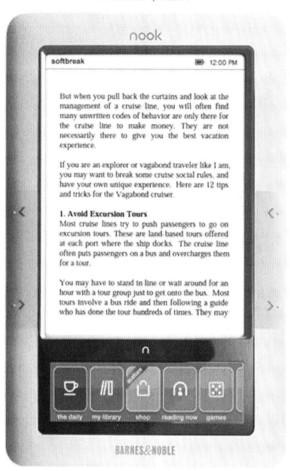

softbreak 🔋 12:00 PM

But when you pull back the curtains and look at the management of a cruise line, you will often find many unwritten codes of behavior are only there for the cruise line to make money. They are not necessarily there to give you the best vacation experience.

If you are an explorer or vagabond traveler like I am, you may want to break some cruise social rules, and have your own unique experience. Here are 12 tips and tricks for the Vagabond cruiser.

1. Avoid Excursion Tours

Most cruise lines try to push passengers to go on excursion tours. These are land based tours offered at each port where the ship docks. The cruise line often puts passengers on a bus and overcharges them for a tour.

You may have to stand in line or wait around for an hour with a tour group just to get onto the bus. Most tours involve a bus ride and then following a guide who has done the tour hundreds of times. They may

< Previous | Next >

Appendix E

Previewing Your Article

There are different ways to preview your article on a Kindle. Since my goal in writing this book is to offer what I think are the easiest ways to get your article published, and without incurring costs, I am going to present three options, and the pros and cons of each.

1) The Amazon Website: When you upload your article on the Amazon (and Nook) website during the publishing process, there is a previewer you can use that Amazon provides. I believe this is the easiest way to preview your document.

You don't have to own a Kindle (or Nook). You can also keep your document in an "editing mode" until you are ready to go live. I prefer previewing my documents this way since the internal links are active, and you can preview what your document will look like on several devices. The only disadvantage is that you cannot check external links to websites.

chance the cruise line owns the jewelry store that they are driving you to.

If you are truly set on an excursion tour, only pick one or two that you absolutely want to go on, or choose one you could never do in the United States. For example, an engineering tour of the Panama Canal is logistically difficult to arrange other than from a cruise.

I strongly believe that by interfacing with communities and foreign cultures on your own, without being separated by the window of a tour bus, is going to give you a much more satisfying travel experience at significantly reduced cost; additionally you'll have unique stories to share with your tablemates.

Photo: Rather than pay $50 for an excursion tour, we hired our own private boat for $10.

2) USB Preview: A second way to preview your article is to physically put your article on your Kindle. You do this by connecting the Kindle to your computer with a USB cable (pull the top off the Kindle electric cord and it will become a USB cable). You drag the converted file into the DOCUMENTS folder of the Kindle.

The benefits of this method are that you can see what your article will actually look like on a real Kindle, and all the links are live. It does require that your document has already been converted into the Amazon format the Kindle can read (see more on document conversion in Appendix F)

3) Use a Previewer: A third way to preview your article is by using "Kindle previewer" software that you can download on your computer for free at http://www.amazon.com/gp/feature.html?ie=UTF8&d ocId=1000234621

This is what the Kindle previewer looks like on your desktop:

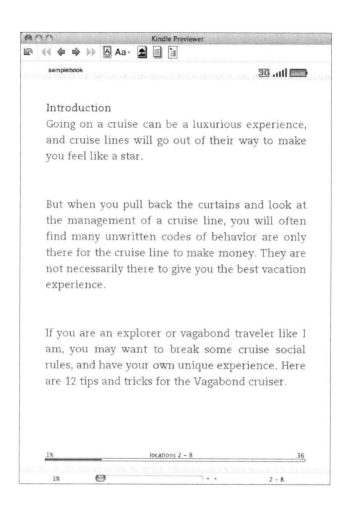

Introduction

Going on a cruise can be a luxurious experience, and cruise lines will go out of their way to make you feel like a star.

But when you pull back the curtains and look at the management of a cruise line, you will often find many unwritten codes of behavior are only there for the cruise line to make money. They are not necessarily there to give you the best vacation experience.

If you are an explorer or vagabond traveler like I am, you may want to break some cruise social rules, and have your own unique experience. Here are 12 tips and tricks for the Vagabond cruiser.

The benefit of this method is that you do not

have to own a Kindle. You can just open your article in the previewer, and I've found it to be very accurate. The cons are that even though the internal bookmark links do work, the external links to websites don't, so you cannot test external links in this previewer. This is similar to the Amazon previewer.

Note: in order to do 2 and 3, you need to convert your document so it is readable on a Kindle. (See instructions in Appendix F below).

As a rule of thumb, no matter which way you prefer to preview your document (Either on Amazon, with preview software, or on an actual Kindle) when you finally upload your document, *always check the Amazon previewer, just to make sure you have uploaded the correct document.*

Amazon's online publishing site assures the author they can move forward in the publishing process without previewing their document, *but never do that*. You should *always preview* anything before you publish it. You don't want someone buying your article only to find you accidentally uploaded your grocery shopping list.

This is something to be particularly aware of when it comes to editing and reposting your article. I frequently update information and links in my articles and I've noticed it is easy to get sloppy and try to rush through an upload when correcting something minor. But as a routine, *always preview your document (in the upload process), before publishing it live.* (see below)

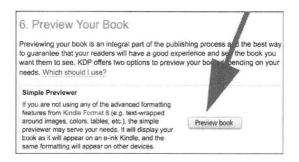

Appendix F

Converting Your Article for Free Through Amazon

There are different ways to convert your document so it is readable on the Kindle. Mobipocket Creator http://www.mobipocket.com/en/downloadsoft/ProductDetailsCreator.asp and Calibre http://calibre-ebook.com/ are often recommended.

I actually prefer another option, which is to convert your document without using conversion software, and instead using Amazon's free conversion service. You will need a kindle to do this. Here are the instructions for converting your article:

1. Find out what your Kindle address is. It can be found on your Kindle under SETTINGS/DEVICE EMAIL or on the Amazon site under MANAGE YOUR KINDLE/KINDLE EMAIL ADDRESS. The address will probably look something like: **johnsmith@Kindle.com**

2. Now exchange the **Kindle.com** part of the address with **@free.Kindle.com**

3.The address will then look like this: **johnsmith@free.Kindle.com** Keep this in your address book for future use.

4. Send your article to this address.

Whenever emailing documents to any kindle, always make sure you have your email address registered as an "approved sender's" address. This is how Amazon prevents people from sending spam to your kindle. Kindles only allow email to come from pre approved email addresses. This comes in handy if you want to send an article to a friend's Kindle.

Registering an "approved sender" email address can be found by following this path on your regular Amazon account where you normally buy books:

Go to:

YOUR ACCOUNT - DIGITAL CONTENT –
MANAGE YOUR KINDLE – MANAGE YOUR
DEVICE – PERSONAL DOCUMENT SETTINGS –
APPROVED PERSONAL DOCUMENT EMAIL
LIST – ADD A NEW APPROVED E-MAIL
ADDRESS.

5. If you have a kindle with wifi, the converted document will go directly to your Kindle through wifi. Otherwise, the document will be returned to you by email. From my experience, it can take 2-5 minutes to get the converted document back, and it usually takes more time for longer documents.

6. If the converted document is returned to you in an email (non-wifi Kindles), it will retain the same name as your original document but the extension will have been replaced. So if your article was saved as **italian_cooking.doc**, it will become **italian_cooking.azw**

7. Click on the link in the email and download it onto your computer.

8. From this point, you can load it onto your

Kindle or look at it through the emulator Kindle Previewer discussed in Appendix E.

~

RESOURCE LIST

Editing

Createspace – Editing for short documents. Createspace is a company owned by Amazon that offers editing services starting around $120 for up 10,000 words.
https://www.createspace.com/pub/services.home.do?tab=PUBLISHING

Books

Smashwords Style Guide - This free ebook will help you through the Smashwords publishing process and teach you how to format documents for their distribution process.
http://www.smashwords.com/books/view/52

Smashwords Book Marketing Guide – This free ebook is the best book I've ever seen on creative ways to market your ebook.
http://www.smashwords.com/books/view/305

Building Your Book for the Kindle – Free ebook published by Amazon that explains basic book formatting.
http://www.amazon.com/dp/B007URVZJ6

Kindle Formatting: The Complete Guide to Formatting Books for the Amazon Kindle by Joshua Tallent - Technical Book by a writer who explains how to format a book in html.

ebook Podcasts

Kindle Chronicles - Best Podcast I know of that covers recent news on anything to do with the Kindle, along with interviews and tips for Kindle readers. This is one of my favorite podcasts. New episode available every Friday.
http://itunes.apple.com/podcast/the-Kindle-chronicles/id286625140

Digital Bookworld Podcast - Information of what's happening in eBook publishing. Podcast is a little

rough (sound wise) but quality of information is top rate.
http://itunes.apple.com/us/podcast/digital-book-world/id357422466

eBook Ninjas - This is a great podcast that talks about the latest news and technology about eBook publishing. Folksy, technical and humorous all at the same time.
http://itunes.apple.com/us/podcast/ebook-ninjas/id287297639

ebook Webcasts

Digital Book World Free Webcasts - Great free webcasts you can sign up for ahead of time that talks about eBook publishing on all kinds of topics.
http://www.digitalbookworld.com/events/webcasts/

O'Reilly Media Webcasts - Dig through their lists of webcasts and you will find ebook publishing topics.
http://oreilly.com/webcasts/

Recommended Blogs

The Passive Voice - All about disruptive changes in the publishing industry, including: self-publishing e-books, e-readers and e-bookstores, emerging legal and contract issues.
http://www.thepassivevoice.com/

Kristine Kathryn Rusch - Excellent blog by best selling author on how to deal with the changes in publishing industry. Check out the series of articles called "Surviving the Transition."
http://kriswrites.com/

Dean Wesley Smith - Best selling author discusses changes in the publishing industry and how to help writers with the new world of publishing. Check out "Killing the Sacred Cows of Publishing" articles.
http://www.deanwesleysmith.com/

Newbie's Guide to Publishing - If you can only read one blog about why you should self-publish ebooks, read this one. The author Joe Konrath is a successful self-publisher on the Kindle and gives all his sales figures upfront. He also requires the same of his guest bloggers. You will get a lot of information on how to market your Kindle publications here.
http://jakonrath.blogspot.com/

EbookNewser – This blog seems has extensive ebook news.

http://www.mediabistro.com/ebooknewser/

ebook Chatter Blog – Free formatting tutorials and news for Ebook Authors
http://ebookchatter.blogspot.com/

Smashwords Blog - Blog written by Mark Coker, owner of the company Smashwords, leader in the independent ebook publishing world.
http://blog.smashwords.com/

Savvy Book Marketer - More of a traditional publishing blog, but great content and tips.
http://bookmarketingmaven.typepad.com/resources/

TheBookDesigner.com - A nice blog on the whole topic of publishing and good design
http://bookdesigner.com/

View from the Publishing Trenches - An author, book designer who writes about publishing.
http://waltshiel.com/

Publishing/Writing: Insights, News, Intrigue - Latest publishing and writing industry insider news.
http://gator1965.wordpress.com/

Self-Publishing Review -
http://www.selfpublishingreview.com/

Kindle Expert (Publishing your content to Kindle) - A Kindle conversion consultant who also writes a blog.
http://www.Kindleexpert.com/

IndieKindle - Stephen Windwalker's resource for authors and indie ebook publishers.
http://indieKindle.blogspot.com/

Ebook Endeavors - An indie fantasy author talks about e-publishing, marketing and blog promotion.
http://www.lindsayburoker.com/

O'Reilly Radar - Not specifically on the topic of Kindle, but a lot of news about on what's going on in publishing.
http://radar.oreilly.com/

Pixel of Ink - I stumbled on this blog, which also has a facebook page, updated by a passionate Kindle reader who searches for free books that come available daily, many that are only free for a short promotional time.
http://www.pixelofink.com/

Kindle Chronicles Blog - The blog associated with the Kindle Chronicles Podcast
http://itunes.apple.com/podcast/the-kindle-

chronicles/id286625140 . I've particularly been impressed by the author who actively responds to emails from readers and listeners. Lots of resources. http://www.theKindlechronicles.com/

Recommended Forums

Amazon Knowledge Base and Community Forums - This is the place where people ask and answer questions about publishing on the Kindle. It's the one place I've found where people know how to solve problems. It's not the best interface, but the content is good. http://forums.Kindledirectpublishing.com/kdpforums/index.jspa

Barnes and Noble Nook Publishing - Where to go to publish your book for the Barnes and Noble Nook. Uploading is quite simple and it has a very clean interface. http://pubit.barnesandnoble.com/pubit_app/bn?t=pi_r eg_home

Barnes and Noble Nook Pubit Help Board - Limited help, but is quite interactive. http://bookclubs.barnesandnoble.com/t5/PubIt-Help-Board/bd-p/pubit

Kindle Formatting Recommendations -Webpage for Amazon publishing guidelines http://forums.Kindledirectpublishing.com/kdpforums/ entry!default.jspa?categoryID=11&externalID=28&fr omSearchPage=true for uploading into an e-Reader.

Kindle Image Formatting Recommendations - Webpage for Amazon image guidelines http://forums.Kindledirectpublishing.com/kdpforums/ entry!default.jspa?categoryID=11&externalID=28&fr omSearchPage=true for uploading into an e-Reader.

Free Software/Blogs

OpenOffice - Software, comparable to Microsoft Office, and includes a word processor http://www.openoffice.org/

Kindle Previewer - Desktop Software to preview your document as if it were on a Kindle http://www.amazon.com/gp/feature.html?ie=UTF8&d ocId=1000234621

Mobipocket Creator Conversion Software (PC) http://www.mobipocket.com/en/downloadsoft/Produc tDetailsCreator.asp

Calibre Conversion Software (MAC)

http://calibre-ebook.com/

Top 10 Free Places to Set Up a Blog
http://sixrevisions.com/tools/top-free-online-blogging/

Articles

How to Begin an Article
http://headrush.typepad.com/creating_passionate_users/2006/10/better_beginnin.HTML

How to End an Article
http://www.smalladdictions.com/Skateboard/articles/NFW-016.htm
http://theadventurouswriter.com/blogwriting/writing-conclusions-how-to-end-your-articles-essays-book-chapters/

Tips for Choosing Effective Tags
http://mlouisalocke.com/2011/10/24/categories-key-words-and-tags-oh-my-why-should-an-author-care/

The Great Digital Land Rush - Publishing
Children's Books on the Nook
http://willterry.blogspot.com/2011/01/great-digital-land-rush.html

Formatting a Comic
http://www.ilovesmashwords.com/2011/05/formattin g-a-graphic-novel-or-comic-book-for-smashwords/

Where to Publish Your Articles

Kindle Direct Publishing
http://kdp.amazon.com/ and KDP Select for book promotion options http://kdp.amazon.com/self-publishing/KDPSelect
If you want a detailed overview of with step-by-step instructions on how to upload your article and fill out the amazon submission form, watch this free amazon video: https://kdp.amazon.com/self-publishing/help?topicId=A2M7MM0UP7PHK0

Kindle "Singles"
How to submit your essay, memoir, reporting and short stories that are between 5,000 and 30,000 words.
http://www.amazon.com/gp/feature.html?ie=UTF8&d ocId=1000700491

Barnes and Noble Pubit
http://www.pubit.barnesandnoble.com/

Smashwords (Distributes your articles to multiple stores such as Apple ibookstore, Sony, Kobo, Diesel, Barnes and Noble and ebook apps. Also offers free ISBN's)
http://www.smashwords.com/

Freebie for my Readers!

I truly value reader feedback. If you have comments, see errors, or are willing to post a review on Amazon, please email me at kateharp@aol.com, and receive a free 20 page PDF on *"Beginner Tips for E-Book Covers: For the Non-Designer."* This is a booklet on how to make your own eBook cover. Thanks! – Kate

How To Write a Review on Amazon

Scroll all the way to the bottom of this page and look for the button that says "Write a customer review":goo.gl/OA8yx

About the Author: *Kate Harper* lives in the San Francisco Bay area and is inspired by the meeting point of art and technology. She is active in the podcasting, art licensing and sharing economy and has designed over 1,000 products for gift industry. See her blog for professional artists and writers at http://kateharperblog.blogspot.com/

Publications for the Creative Person

How to Make an EBook Cover for Non-Designers is an illustrated book will show you how to make your own e-book cover, even if you are not a designer. For the indie writer who is on a budget and wants to publish and sell their own book in online stores like Amazon.com and the Apple iBookstore. eBook covers should be designed differently than printed book covers in order to make them stand out in online bookstores. Learn how to design a basic book cover by using step-by-step visual instructions, and to size a digital file to upload into an eBook store.

20 Steps to Art Licensing is a book about how to license you
art to companies that publish greeting cards, or manufacture
coffee mugs, magnets, wall hangings, kitchen items, and dozens
of other gift items. Learn how to prepare your art, what
companies to contact, how to find agents, and what trade shows
to attend. Includes extensive resources on social media,
copyrights, licensing community groups, and lists of interviews
with professional designers

7 Mistakes Greeting Card Writers Make is a booklet that explains what to avoid when submitting greeting card verse to publishers. Learn how to create a trendy card that reflects the contemporary world we live in, and how to use your own personal experience to create card verse. Topics include: how to avoid limiting your market, when to use adjectives, not creating card for enemies, write like people talk and a list of why card sentiment submissions are often rejected. You can increase your odds of success by 60% just by doing a few simple things. Includes a list of card publishers and their guidelines, links to writer interviews, and writing exercises for how to create good verse.

Unusual Ways to Market Greeting Cards, and 22 places to get your designs featured is a booklet on how to get your cards noticed in non-traditional ways. Everything from why you should send cards to your dentist, to how to get a special feature in national publication. Great tips for designers who are starting out and want to get their cards into the hands of people beyond friends and family. *Special Section:* 22 Gift Industry Trade Publications who seek out new greeting card designs and feature artists for free.

Get Your Greeting Cards into Stores explains how to sell cards nationwide. Included are detailed guidelines on: How to price cards for a profit, get professional feedback, find sales representatives and follow industry standards. Information is also applicable to gift items, magnets, journals, calendars, collectibles, etc.

Funny Kid Quotes: Advice for the Office is an illustrated art booklet of children's quotes for the workplace, designed by artist Kate Harper. These quotes are not your typical "sweet" messages, rather, they push the edge with statements such as ,"You know it was a good day if you didn't hit or bite anyone." (-Nathanial, age 4) and ,"If you'd just do what I tell you, I wouldn't have to be so bossy" (-Addison, age 4). Also includes 30 Free Ready-To-Print posters to hang on the wall.

Peer-to-Peer Sharing Directory explains how to use the social web and mobile apps to swap clothes, find a taxi mate, rent out parking space, or lead our own specialized tour that goes off the beaten path. This guide is a list of peer-to-peer networks that: Exchange goods or services, are conducted through a website or mobile app, allows the recipient to save money, and the giver to make money from underutilized goods.

18184626R00074

Made in the USA
Middletown, DE
24 February 2015